ALSO BY DAVID GETZ,
WITH ILLUSTRATIONS
BY PETER McCARTY

FROZEN MAN

PURPLE DEATH

FROZEN GIRL

FROZEN GIRL

THE DISCOVERY OF AN INCAN MUMMY

DAVID GETZ

ILLUSTRATIONS BY
PETER McCARTY

SQUARE
FISH

HENRY HOLT AND COMPANY · NEW YORK

Thanks to the following people for the time in personal interviews they gave me: Bill Conklin, Edward McCarthy, Craig Morris, Jane Pratt, Johan Reinhard, and John Verano.

For the girls: for our ecstatic Edyn, who could laugh down any volcano; for her cousin, Emily, the exquisite; for Emma and Molly, the country mice; for Maxine, who continues to conquer one peak after another; for Jaqui, my navigator.

And hey, let's hear it for the guy, Bobby Stark, engineer of this adventure.   —D. G.

To Yunhee   —P. M.

SQUARE
FISH

An imprint of Macmillan Publishing Group, LLC
175 Fifth Avenue, New York, NY 10010
mackids.com

FROZEN GIRL. Text copyright © 1998 by David Getz.
Illustrations copyright © 1998 by Peter McCarty.

Square Fish and the Square Fish logo are trademarks of Macmillan and
are used by Henry Holt and Company under license from Macmillan.

Our books may be purchased in bulk for promotional, educational, or business use. Please contact your local
bookseller or the Macmillan Corporate and Premium Sales Department at (800) 221-7945 ext. 5442 or by e-mail
at MacmillanSpecialMarkets@macmillan.com.

Library of Congress Cataloging-in-Publication Data
Getz, David. Frozen girl / by David Getz: Illustrations by Peter McCarty.
p.   cm.
Summary: Discusses the discovery, history, and significance of an Incan mummy
found frozen in the mountains of Peru.

1. Incas—Antiquities—Juvenile literature. 2. Mummies—Peru—Ampato, Mount—Juvenile literature. 3. Incas—
Social life and customs—Juvenile literature. 4. Archaeology—Methodology—Juvenile literature. 5. Peru—
Antiquities—Juvenile literature. [1. Incas—Antiquities. 2. Indians of South America—Antiquities. 3. Excavations
(Archaeology)—Peru. 4. Archaeology. 5. Peru—Antiquities.] I. McCarty, Peter, ill. II. Title.
F3429.3.M8G47   1998   985'.019—dc2li   97-40643

ISBN 978-1-250-14363-1 (paperback)

Originally published in the United States by Henry Holt and Company
First Square Fish edition, 2018
Square Fish logo designed by Filomena Tuosto

1   3   5   7   9   10   8   6   4   2

Contents

FROZEN GIRL

The Climb

He had just wanted to get a closer look at an awakened volcano.

In 1990, the volcano Nevado Sabancaya in the Peruvian Andes began erupting, belching mile-high mushroom clouds that stank of rotten eggs. Though no lava flowed, volcanic ash rained for miles over the surrounding peaks. The dark ash absorbed heat. For the first time in hundreds of years, the thick ice coating the mountains began to melt.

As an archaeologist and mountain climber, Johan Reinhard wanted to get up there and have a look around. By climbing nearby Mount Ampato, the tallest mountain in the region, he could look down on smoking Sabancaya.

Reinhard had spent the past sixteen years studying how people lived within the Andes Mountains. He had scaled over a hundred peaks. Diving for artifacts in Lake Titicaca, the highest lake in the world, he had been attacked by smugglers. Yet none of these experiences would equal the adventure he was about to have.

"I was just curious," Reinhard says. "The last thing I expected to find was the frozen body of a girl sacrificed five hundred years ago."

Reinhard and his climbing partner, Miguel Zarate, reached Cabanoconde, the Peruvian village nearest Ampato, in early September 1995. The villagers were engaged in a festival to celebrate the first planting. They poured chicha, a beer made from corn, onto the ground to thank Pachamama, the earth goddess. They blew coca leaves toward the mountain gods. Ampato was one of those gods. It sent down fresh water for drinking and irrigation. It provided grass for the llamas to graze.

Reinhard and Zarate participated in the festival. They, too, blew coca leaves toward Ampato. They asked it to let them enter its realm and return safely.

Though Reinhard doesn't believe the mountains are gods, he believes it is important to approach a mountain with the same respect a local villager would show. He works hard to think of the mountain as a living being, not some lifeless object to be conquered. This approach calms him. If he doesn't discover something on a climb, he is not exasperated.

"You get what the mountain wants to give you," Reinhard says.

At first Ampato didn't seem welcoming. As Reinhard and Zarate looked for an easier route to the summit, they came upon a field of jagged ice sticking up from the ground like the stalagmites of a cave. The dark ash from Sabancaya had partially melted the thick ice that once covered the ground. What was once as smooth and easy to cross as a frozen pond now resembled a dirty gray landscape of icy knives, swords, and pickets called penatente. The climbers broke and crashed their way up through this penatente for hours. Then, at an altitude of 20,400 feet, they noticed something strange.

Just above eye level, the ice was streaked with grass. It was a wild grass called ichu. Ichu doesn't grow above 15,000 feet. Yet they were surrounded by it.

What's going on here? Reinhard wondered.

Exploring the area where the ice had melted, Reinhard and Zarate soon came upon wood, which also didn't belong this high up the mountain, well above where trees could grow. Some of the wood was charred, as if it had been used for campfires. They found the remains of poles. They also discovered flat stones. One had a rope tied around it, as if it had been dragged up to this height.

"We knew we were on to something," Reinhard recalls.

Pottery lay everywhere. They found bits of clothing, remains of sacks, and four or five sandals. Some of the sandals had been made of woven grass with wool for straps. They found a leather moccasin.

Reinhard recognized the style of the clothing and the pottery. They were from the Incas. Sometime in the 1400s, the Incas began to conquer one state in the Andes after another until they ruled an empire that spanned nearly the entire western length of South America. Governing from Cuzco, the Incas controlled the lives of over twenty million people. Then, in 1532, the Spanish, led by Francisco Pizarro, began the conquest and destruction of the empire.

Reinhard and Zarate had discovered an Inca campsite that had been hidden under thick ice for almost five hundred years.

The flat rocks, Reinhard reasoned, must have served as flooring for the camp. The grass was probably used as carpeting to cover the cold, cold ground. They found llama feces. Llamas were probably used to help carry supplies.

Reinhard estimates it must have taken fifty to one hundred men weeks, going up and down the mountain, to transport all of that grass and wood to prepare the camp. "It didn't take a genius to realize we were at an important site," Reinhard said.

But why had the Incas camped at this height?

Where were they going?

To the Summit

We were at 20,400 feet, and for people to be camping up there meant they had to go somewhere else. Where were they going? Reinhard wondered.

Ampato's mountaintop is a collapsed volcanic crater shaped like the opened mouth of some mythical giant, with broken ridges for teeth. Reinhard and Zarate stood at the bottom of that jaw, looking toward Ampato's highest point. "The summit looked pretty impressive from where we were," Reinhard remembers.

But it was getting late.

It was 4:30 P.M. and it would be dark in little more than an hour. They had to turn around and head back down to their base camp. As they began their descent,

Reinhard surveyed the mountain for the best route for tomorrow's climb to the summit. Looking through his binoculars, he spotted a small structure on level ground. He couldn't tell what it was, but its rectangular shape was in the style of Inca structures.

Tomorrow they would move their tent, their supplies, and their stove to that site to use it as a temporary base before making their final ascent.

The next morning, they moved their supplies to their new site at 19,200 feet. The summit was within striking distance. Exploring this new area, Reinhard and Zarate discovered more Inca artifacts, including tent poles and a stone wall platform two feet high and with an area of five hundred square feet.

Reinhard marveled at the Incas' labor. Presented with a mountain peak as barren as the moon, the Incas had carried, from miles away, stones for floors, tons of grass for carpeting, wood for tents, and countless other materials to build a series of campsites leading up to the summit. They had even carved a trail into the mountain's face and lined it with wood and grass.

But why?

The next day, September 8, Reinhard and Zarate reached Ampato's summit. It was a steep and tiny ridge about three feet across. In 1993, Carlos Zarate, Miguel's brother, had reported that the summit was thirty feet across and covered in ice. Sometime in the two years since then, the ash from Sabancaya had melted the ice and caused the ridge to collapse.

After finding no new discoveries, and just about ready to begin the descent, Reinhard began to make notes about the climb. Zarate kept moving and exploring. Reinhard recorded the altitude of the summit, wrote down the time, and described the route of their ascent. Suddenly, Zarate whistled. He held up his ice ax. Reinhard looked down. Rising up from the ground was a crown of red feathers.

Reinhard and Zarate had seen similar feathers before, in the headdresses of small Inca statues. Reinhard tied a rope around Zarate and lowered him down the dangerously steep slope. Working carefully, Zarate removed a small statue, then two more. The figurines— one gold, one silver, and one made of rare spondylus shells found off the coast of Ecuador—were all dressed in beautiful Inca fabrics. Each had been buried facing Ampato's summit.

"It was like a gift," Reinhard says. The statues were in loose rock, ready to fall down the slope at any moment.

Ampato was being kind.

▶ *One of the miniature idols found on Mount Ampato near the frozen girl. The idol is made of gold and its clothes are copies of what Inca women wore more than five hundred years ago.* COPYRIGHT BILL CONKLIN

"Then I started thinking like a scientist," Reinhard recalls. He needed to record the location of their discoveries. Unfortunately, he had forgotten his compass. So he had to determine where they were and where the statues had been located by figuring out where the sun rose and set at that time of the year, and where he knew the village was. He checked everything against a map.

Looking around, he saw large stones that were probably once part of another structure. The rest of it must have collapsed as the ridge collapsed. Where had the rest of the structure gone? Had other valuable artifacts tumbled down the mountain along with the stones of the structure?

"I had a brilliant idea," Reinhard says. "And if you remember your name at 21,000 feet, you're brilliant."

There were two gullies, paths carved out by melted snow running down the mountain. Reinhard wrapped two stones in yellow plastic and threw them down the gullies. Perhaps one of the wrapped rocks would follow the same path as the missing parts of the structure. Reinhard and Zarate climbed down the slope after their tumbling yellow rocks.

One rock had stopped where the slope met sharp eroded ice. Just beyond, the two climbers noticed a bundle of cloth.

Instantly, both men recognized the bundle. Controlling their emotions, they refused to say aloud what they knew.

"Maybe it's a climber's backpack," Zarate offered.

"It doesn't look like any climber's backpack I've ever seen," Reinhard said.

Getting closer, Reinhard and Zarate no longer had any doubt. They had come upon an Inca mummy bundle, the textile-covered body of a human sacrifice. Both climbers had seen mummy bundles before. They knew that within those Inca textiles was the body of someone who had been killed as an offering to the gods.

Scattered about the body were pieces of cloth, llama bones, fragments of pottery, and two cloth bags containing corn kernels and a corncob. There was also another figurine, made of shell.

Reinhard recorded the location of this discovery, then took some photos. He then went to help Zarate lift the body. They couldn't move it. The ice surrounding the fabric had melted, then refrozen to the mountain.

After some struggle, Zarate eventually freed the body from the surrounding ice. As Reinhard helped him get a better grip, they turned the body on its side. The cloth covering its face fell open. Suddenly, they found themselves looking into the face of some-one dead.

"I saw a dried face of what looked to be a female," Reinhard says. "She even had some of her eyelashes and eyebrows. But her teeth were very prominent be-cause her lips had dried back. You were looking at teeth. It was like a little thing from the creep show." Recovering from the shock, Reinhard began to think clearly. He had a decision to make.

Descent

Reinhard and Zarate were suddenly confronted by a dilemma. They had discovered the body of a female who had died and been buried five hundred years ago. Except for her face, her body appeared frozen. Freezing stops decay. If this girl were frozen at the time of death, her body could be remarkably well preserved. Scientists could examine her and learn about her health almost as well as a doctor could learn about the health of a living patient.

Would removing her body offend the people of the nearby villages? Would Reinhard and Zarate be considered grave robbers? Reinhard considered the situation. The body, he reasoned, had already been removed from its grave when the summit collapsed. If he and Zarate left it there, it would be exposed to the wind, the snow, volcanic ash, sun, lightning, or an avalanche.

"We knew we were doing no good by letting it be destroyed by the natural environment," Reinhard says. They also knew that once their expedition got back and word spread about the artifacts, treasure hunters, called huaqueros, would eventually find the body. Huaqueros made money by illegally selling artifacts and archaeological treasures.

"There were a lot of things I had to think of," Reinhard says. "I decided the best thing to do was to take the body right then and there if I could."

It was at this point that Reinhard was struck with diarrhea. He had drunk melted snow that had minerals in it from the volcanic ash. The diarrhea didn't last long, but it made him feel terrible. He already felt weak. Neither he nor Zarate had eaten all day because the climb had taken longer than they expected. Still, Reinhard was determined to bring the body down from the mountain.

And he had to do it before it began to thaw. If the descent took too long, and the body began to warm, it would begin to decay like a piece of meat left out in the sun.

Reinhard gave Zarate his supplies and water, his camera, and other things to carry. He kept the gold, silver, and spondylus figurines, cushioned with spare clothing, in the top pockets of his backpack. He and Zarate then wedged the bottom of the mummy bundle into the lower section of his backpack and strapped the rest of it to the outside.

The burden was so heavy he could barely stand up. Zarate had to help him. Stepping up over anything was nearly impossible. Climbing through and over the penatente was exhausting. The ground was covered with volcanic ash and scree—loose, slippery rocks. Reinhard fell time and time again.

"Every time I slipped, I went down like a sack of potatoes," he recalls.

Every fall knocked the wind out of him. It was excruciating. There were places where Zarate had to carve steps in the ice.

They reached the crater's edge by 6:15 P.M. It was dark and there was no moon. It was snowing lightly. The slope was steep, covered in ice and more scree. Wearing headlamps, Reinhard and Zarate continued their painful descent. At times they had to stop so Zarate could carve more footholds for Reinhard. Zarate pleaded for Reinhard to leave the mummy behind. He knew that if Reinhard began to slide, the two of them would be swept down the mountain.

Even with the headlamps, they could no longer see where they were going. Finally, down to 20,000 feet, Reinhard and Zarate wedged the mummy into a gully and returned to their base camp.

The next morning, Reinhard went back up for the mummy as Zarate took their gear and tent and went down to a lower camp to get help.

The climb in the daytime was easier, but it was still an incredible labor. The weight of the mummy on his back was exhausting. Reinhard knew that if he fell and injured himself now, he would be alone for hours until Zarate found him.

"There were many times when I fell and said, 'That's it! I can't go any farther!' And then I'd get my breath back, and feel my body get a little strength back, and I'd go on again."

The wind changed. It began to blow volcanic ash directly into his face and mouth. Already struggling to get enough air into his lungs, Reinhard was now breathing volcanic ash.

That afternoon Zarate arrived and was able to take the mummy off Reinhard's back and carry her down to a camp where a man was waiting with two burros.

They stopped that night at a muddy stream, where they fed the burros.

The following morning they woke up at dawn. They knew there was a bus that left at eleven that evening from Cabanoconde to Arequipa, where there was a university and a place to care for the mummy. They decided to go for it.

They wrapped the still-frozen mummy in two insulation pads from their sleeping bags. This would keep it at a fairly even temperature. Even though the sun was out, they were still at 14,300 feet, where it was cold. They placed the bundle on the back of a burro. The burro driver removed a cloth and covered the burro's eyes.

If the burro knew it was carrying a dead body, the driver explained, it would panic and flee.

"So we got it on the burro and took off," Reinhard says. "We had one ten-minute break to split up a can of tuna amongst the three of us. And then we continued on. It was a thirteen-hour-straight walk."

It was a black night, without a moon. When they reached the last leg of their descent, the batteries for their headlamps were dying. They still had a zigzag trail that wound 3,500 feet down to the village. Though the men could not see more than a few feet in front of them, the burros knew the way and led them safely into Cabanoconde by nine o'clock that evening.

They placed the wrapped, still-frozen mummy in a storage compartment under the bus, far from the engine. Zarate climbed aboard. Reinhard went to his room to get some sleep.

By the following morning, the mummy was safe in a refrigerated case at Catholic University in Arequipa, Peru. Somewhere along the way, she had acquired a name. She was now known as Juanita.

A Frozen Message

The message to Bill Conklin came in on his E-mail at the National Gallery of Art in Washington, D.C. Could he come down to Peru? The clothed, frozen body of an Inca girl had been discovered high up on Mount Ampato. Two more bodies of children had been found on a follow-up expedition. Bill Conklin is an expert on the textiles, the woven fabrics, of the Andes. The message was from Sonia Guillen, who was directing the research on Juanita at Catholic University in Arequipa. Guillen had spoken with other researchers who felt that Juanita's textiles needed to be removed to preserve both her clothing and her body.

He had to come within ten days.

The Incas and the people who lived in the Andes before them never developed a system of writing. Textiles took the place of books. Colors, materials, patterns, and symbols took the place of words. Textiles were an important form of communication, similar to our flags, money, passports, or religious objects.

"They told a person, 'This is where I'm from. This is my village. This is what I believe. This is my rank in society. These are the gods I believe in.' All of this," Bill Conklin explains, "would have been readable from the garments."

What Juanita wore could tell us who she was. Most people who lived in the Inca empire were not Incas. They were peasants or artisans from different states of the empire. The Incas were just one group, the ruling tribe, the elite that imposed their laws, religion, and customs on everyone else. Only Incas were allowed to wear Inca textiles. If Juanita were dressed in the clothing of Incas, what did that tell us about her life? What could it tell about the Incas?

Though a fully dressed Inca female had never been discovered, Conklin had some idea of what Inca females wore from drawings and writings done after the Spanish conquest. Conklin knew that all females wore an aksu, a woven rectangular garment, as their main article of clothing. This was wrapped like a bath towel over the body. The corners were crossed in the back, drawn up over the shoulders, and held down in front with decorative pins called tupus. A lliclla (pronounced yick-ya) was a shawl worn over the shoulders and fastened in the front by another tupu.

Is this how Juanita would be dressed?

Conklin was eager to get down to Peru to find out. What did her textiles look like? How well were they preserved? Were they in danger of falling apart?

Of course, he would go. Ten days! Conklin immediately began to do some research. Fortunately, the National Gallery received books from all over the world. He read everything there was to read on frozen textiles. He talked to textile conservators—experts who restore, preserve, and study textiles—from the Smithsonian Museum, the American Museum of Natural History, the National Gallery, and other museums.

"But then I thought I'd better get some hands-on experience."

Conklin knew that Juanita's clothing was made from the wool of the alpaca, an Andean relative of the llama. What happened to alpaca wool when it froze?

It so happened that Conklin had a pair of alpaca gloves at home. He soaked one glove in water, kept

the other dry, and put them both in his home freezer. Would either glove be damaged by the cold? Would either be damaged when it was warmed up again? Would the dry glove survive any differently than the wet glove?

Waiting for his gloves to freeze, Conklin thought of the alpaca, living high up in the mountains. It gets terribly cold up there at night, Conklin realized. When the alpaca lies down to sleep, its outer fur must freeze. In the warmer daytime, that fur must thaw. If freezing and thawing are part of an alpaca's life, freezing and thawing shouldn't hurt alpaca textiles.

Conklin removed his gloves from the freezer. He let each thaw and examined their fibers under a microscope. Both gloves were just fine. He repeated his experiment a number of times. As he expected, freezing and thawing had no bad effects on the material. This was confirmed by the experts from other museums.

It was exciting news. Juanita's clothing could be thawed without damaging the material. Once removed from her body, her clothing could be restored to its original beauty.

But there were problems.

Juanita's body was well preserved because it was frozen. Unlike alpaca gloves, Juanita's body would be irreversibly damaged if it was thawed. Researchers were keeping Juanita's body in a freezer in Arequipa at a temperature between zero and seven degrees Fahrenheit. Nobody was allowed to take it out to examine it for more than thirty minutes at a time.

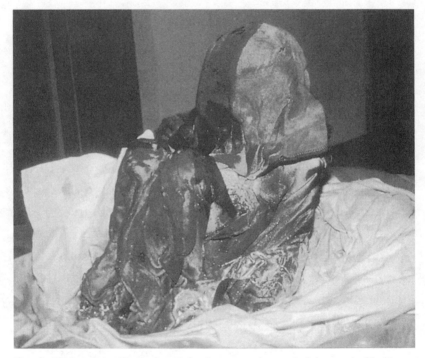

► *The frozen girl, or "Juanita," wasn't the only mummy on the mountain. Other mummies, like this young girl, were found buried near Juanita. This girl was probably sacrificed at the same time as Juanita.* COPYRIGHT BILL CONKLIN

How could Bill Conklin thaw Juanita's clothing without thawing her body? Much of the clothing was frozen to her skin. Could Conklin help researchers remove her textiles without damaging Juanita's skin?

Juanita would not be obliging. She was frozen solid. Her body was acting like an eighty-pound chunk of ice. She cooled anything that came in contact with her.

Making matters worse, Juanita's textiles were a jumbled mess of wrinkles and folds about her. "It was like looking into a washing machine after the clothing had tumbled," Conklin explains.

Talking back and forth with Sonia Guillen in Peru, Bill Conklin came up with a plan.

A Remarkable Textile

We had to develop a technique to heat locally, conservatively, and safely," Bill Conklin explained.

Conklin came up with a plan that was cheap, yet effective. Why not heat small cotton towels and place them on Juanita's frozen textiles? Heat would travel from the towel to the textile. The textile would melt and the towel would absorb the water. Square foot by square foot, Juanita's outer textiles could be thawed. Conklin E-mailed this idea down to Peru.

When he arrived, he was delighted to see his towel technique in use. Six people were involved in the procedure of heating cotton towels with hair dryers, pressing the towels onto the frozen textiles, thawing the materials, and mopping up the water. It was working wonderfully. Guillen and her researchers used temperature probes to carefully monitor the effects of keeping the bodies out of their refrigerated containers. At the beginning, they worked a half hour a day, one body at a time. This was excruciatingly slow. Gradually, watching the probes, they were able to work for longer time periods without damaging the bodies.

But the deep folds in Juanita's clothing presented a problem. There were wrinkles and crevices that couldn't be reached with the towels. Somebody suggested using a soldering iron, an electric device with a pointed metal rod that is used to melt a metal alloy to join metal surfaces. Quietly, Conklin panicked.

Could the material be thawed safely with the iron? Conklin didn't like the idea. He froze one of the cotton towels, then placed the heated soldering iron against the frozen towel. Instantly, the rod burned the fabric, destroying it.

Conklin and the other researchers came up with a better plan. They placed warm water in plastic bags, sealed them, and placed them in the crevices. It worked. More of the textiles thawed.

Still, more problems arose. Sometime after Sabancaya erupted, the ledge on which Juanita was buried collapsed, causing her to tumble down the mountain for two hundred yards. As she fell, she accumulated snow, which melted and refroze in different folds in her clothing. How could these be melted?

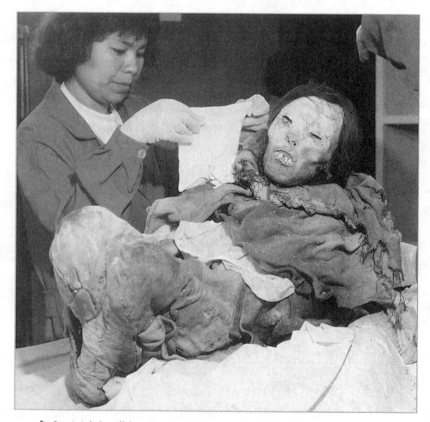

► *Juanita's body, still frozen, awaits examination. Small white towels are heated and then placed on the body to slowly thaw out the frozen textiles wrapped around her.* COPYRIGHT BILL CONKLIN

Conklin developed the technique of filling hypodermic syringes with distilled water and injecting the water into the frozen snow, then absorbing the melted snow with paper towels. This was also successful.

Over three trips down to Peru for ten days each time, Conklin helped Sonia Guillen and the other researchers remove Juanita's lliclla.

"It's a remarkable textile, complete and in excellent condition, intact in every way. Marvelous patterning, beautifully woven," Conklin said.

They couldn't remove her aksu and her belt. Juanita's frozen hand still grips portions of that material very firmly. "And we haven't figured out a way to separate them," Conklin says, "though I'm sure we will."

The clothing Juanita wore was brilliantly colored in gold, red, white, and purple. Her lliclla, her aksu, and her other garments were the royal or official Inca garments. They were probably woven in the Inca capital of Cuzco. Chroniclers write of acclas, places where young girls were kept to weave garments for the Incas. Though Inca garments, like bath towels, weren't sized to fit individuals, Conklin says Juanita's clothing was intentionally large for her. The Incas didn't look at death as the end of someone's existence.

Death was thought to be a gate someone passed through on the way to another state of being. Perhaps, Conklin reasons, Juanita's clothing was large on her because the Incas expected her to grow as she continued on to the next part of her existence after death.

Just as revealing as her beautiful garments were the drab ones that were torn from her body as she tumbled down the mountain. These consisted of the same items as her official garments, but were gray and simple. They must have been used as an outer wrapper

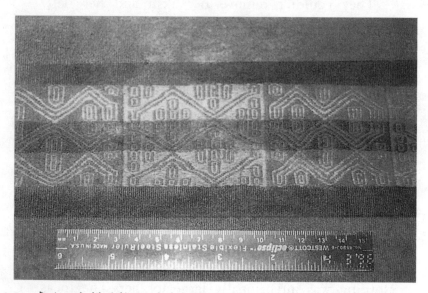

► *A sample of the clothing worn by the frozen girl at the time of her sacrifice. All the textiles she wore were specially made for her and were very elaborate.* COPYRIGHT BILL CONKLIN

over her sacrificial clothing. Attached to this outer wrapping was a small cloth bag, which held personal items, such as a piece of shell on a string, and some hair clippings, which were probably Juanita's. It was (and still is) a Peruvian custom to keep the clippings from a child's first haircut. Conklin believes these outer garments were Juanita's own clothes. They show signs of repair.

"You look at the darning," Conklin says, "and you see the evidence of the handiwork. It gives you some feeling for her. It was probably her own work. She probably repaired her own clothes."

If she repaired her own clothes, Conklin says, she was probably not a member of the royalty. Most likely she was a village girl who was picked to be sacrificed because of her beauty. Many writers after the conquest described how the Incas searched for children without blemishes or marks or deformities to be sacrificed to the gods. The gods were all-knowing and all-powerful. The Incas would only offer them physically perfect gifts.

"It was a great honor to be selected for sacrifice," says Craig Morris, an expert on the Incas from the American Museum of Natural History. "It would not have been a sudden thing. It was something that

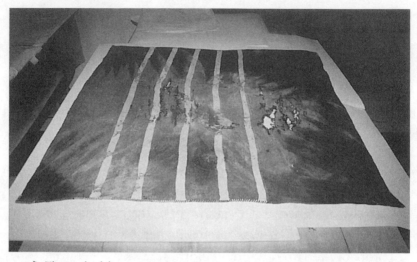

► *The outer shawl that was wrapped around Juanita was her own. It was a simple gray and white textile with no decoration.* COPYRIGHT BILL CONKLIN

would have been known for weeks and months, if not longer than that. And certainly toward the end, there would have been feasts. She would have been very well treated."

Juanita's clothing, her own textiles placed over her Inca textiles, tell a Cinderella-type story. When the Incas chose Juanita to be sacrificed, they transformed her from an ordinary girl into royalty. The clothes she wore to her death were the clothes of a princess.

A Child of the Andes

We will never know who she really was, or what her childhood was like. Since there was no written language before the Spanish conquest, there is no written record of Juanita's childhood, her selection for sacrifice, or her last day. Her thoughts, her experiences, her real name will never be learned.

What we have instead are glimpses of everyday life in the Inca empire from the chroniclers. These authors could only write their accounts after the conquest, when Spain introduced the Spanish written language into Peru. The chroniclers included Spanish soldiers, Spanish priests, and other travelers.

As the Spanish took over Peru, they abused its people, stole its riches, and sought to destroy its culture.

Taking all the golden statues and ornaments they could find, they robbed the Incas of an estimated twenty million dollars in gold. They destroyed many Inca buildings. They banned many religious customs, including sacrifices. They made many social customs illegal. The Spanish rulers would not allow a Peruvian woman to wear an aksu because it showed too much of her legs. Before the conquest, many Peruvians who believed the mountains were their ancestors would press boards against their newborn babies' soft heads to shape them to resemble their sacred peaks. The Spanish made this custom a crime.

The new government awarded important Spaniards Peruvian land, along with the people living on it. Many Peruvians were forced to work as slaves on farms or in the dangerous mines. Many Peruvians escaped the country to live away from the Spanish. Many others died from the diseases the conquerors brought with them from Spain.

The Spanish changed the way Peruvians lived, farmed, worshiped, and dressed. As a result, the customs that the chroniclers wrote about had already begun to disappear. Many authors had to rely on Incas or common people to get an idea of what life was like before the conquest. Since the people interviewed could not refer to books or papers, they had to rely on their memories, or the stories told by their parents or grandparents. As a result, what the chroniclers wrote, and what we know about the Incas, is not always accurate. Many chroniclers simply made things up to make their stories more dramatic or to make the Incas look better or worse. This makes the truth even more difficult to come by.

How do we know when Juanita was sacrificed?

We know the artifacts found with her belonged to the Incas. We know from the chronicles that the Incas had conquered the area where Juanita was sacrificed sometime around 1470. As Dr. Craig Morris says, "And most of those things are not absolutely certain, to be honest." That places her sacrifice sometime after 1470 and before the 1530s. There is no scientific dating technique, such as carbon 14, that will give a more accurate time of death.

But what about Juanita? Who was she?

If she was an ordinary child, we can only guess at what her life was like from reading the chroniclers' accounts of childhood in the Andes.

Her pregnant mother probably worked until the very last minute, giving birth to Juanita with the help of neighbors. There were no special professions, no doctors or midwives that helped with births. Immediately after birth, her mother washed both herself and her infant in a cold stream. She then wrapped Juanita tightly in swaddling blankets and placed her in a cradle. She may have unwrapped these blankets at night, exposing Juanita to the cold, damp air. This was thought to toughen children, making them more capable of surviving the harsh life of the mountains. Soon, her mother got back to work, spinning and weaving, caring for her children, preparing meals and farming.

Juanita's arms were kept within these swaddling blankets for her first three months. Her mother believed that to remove them sooner would make the baby's arms grow weak. The cradle was built like a bench with four legs. It could be carried or just as easily be put down. One leg of the cradle was shorter than the others so that it could be rocked to lull the baby to sleep.

The family probably grew corn or potatoes, or tended alpacas or llamas. They couldn't own their own land. All the land, animals, and plants belonged to the ruling Incas. To some extent, so did the people. The Incas could move entire families away from their homes and force them to settle in newly conquered

areas. They could take men from their families and force them to work constructing forts, roads, or temples. The Inca also took young girls from families to work making textiles in the acclas. They could also take a child to be sacrificed to the gods.

Juanita's family probably lived in a simple hut with a thatched roof. It was probably sooty and smelly, with guinea pigs and dogs living inside. The guinea pigs were raised for food. Juanita's diet would also include dried llama meat, corn, and potatoes. Potatoes were dried and crushed into a white meal, called chuno. The family sat on the floor for two meals a day, eating stews or soups from bowls. They also made and drank their own chicha.

The people of the Inca empire lived in a world of spirits. A statue of their household god was placed within a niche on the wall. Outside, spirits lived within the rocks, caves, soil, and streams. When farming, Juanita's parents poured chicha on the ground to satisfy the earth goddess. They prayed when crossing rivers, and left stones or small personal objects on mountain passes. The mountain gods controlled their lives, sending down water, making the weather, and sometimes punishing them with avalanches, storms, earthquakes, or volcanoes.

When Juanita turned two, she was weaned from her mother's milk. Her family held a feast, drinking, dancing, and laughing. Her eldest uncle cut her hair and her nails, which were kept. The small cloth bag Juanita was buried with contained hair clippings probably from this ceremony. It was also at this time that Juanita was given her first official name.

These names often referred to some animal or place or object from nature. Some names for girls were Star, Gold, Egg, or Coca. She kept this name until she was a young teen. She would never have been called Juanita. Juanita is a Spanish name.

At the end of the ceremony, her relatives gave her presents. They prayed to the gods she would live a long life.

"The Healthiest Teeth
I've Ever Seen"

She was killed between her twelfth and thirteenth birthdays.

"We can estimate age very accurately with dental X rays," John Verano explains. Verano is a physical anthropologist, a person who studies the skeletons of ancient people to learn about their lives. He has also studied Juanita.

The teeth of a healthy child develop according to a dependable schedule. Each tooth grows its crown, then its roots, and then breaks through the gums at a predictable time in a child's life. By looking at X rays of a child's jaw to see which teeth are still developing under the gums and which are emerging, scientists can determine a child's age to within one year.

Juanita's second molars, which erupt at twelve, were in place. Her wisdom teeth, which erupt at thirteen, were not.

Researchers also studied X rays of Juanita's skeleton.

At the end of a growing child's long bones is a growth center called the epiphysis. When a child is still growing, this end part is separated from the main bone by cartilage. Epiphyses unite with long bones when a child stops growing, sometime between the ages of fifteen and eighteen. Since different epiphyses unite at different times in a child's life, scientists can examine them in X rays to get a good estimate of a child's age. Though epiphysis X rays are not as accurate as dental X rays, they helped confirm that Juanita died sometime before her thirteenth birthday.

Further examinations indicated that she had begun to develop breasts. Juanita had probably reached puberty. Chroniclers write that a great feast was held for girls at the onset of puberty. This would have begun with Juanita staying in her house for three days, fasting. On the third day, she was allowed to eat raw corn. On the following day, her mother washed her and dressed her in new clothes and white sandals, then presented her to her relatives, who were waiting outside. Her most important uncle then gave her a new name. Her relatives gave her presents. Perhaps one of those presents was the shell she carried in her bag.

Studies of her teeth and dental X rays showed that she had lived a healthy life. Dr. Elliot Fishman, a radiologist at Johns Hopkins University, said, "Juanita had the healthiest teeth I've ever seen." There was no evidence of gum or tooth disease caused by malnutrition. There were no growth arrest lines on either Juanita's teeth or bones. If a child experiences a severe illness or periods of starvation, the bones and teeth will stop growing. When the illness or malnutrition passes, growth begins anew, leaving a visible line on the teeth and gums.

"She appears to have been in excellent health," adds Dr. Edward McCarthy. McCarthy is a pathologist, a doctor who studies the effects of diseases on people. "The overall amount of tissue on her body seems to be pretty good," McCarthy says. Judging from her frozen body, she probably weighed between eighty and ninety pounds. Measurements indicate she was no taller than five foot one.

"Apparently," John Verano says, "she lived at a time when food was abundant and people were doing pretty well."

Unfortunately, she is no longer physically perfect. Her body was not perfectly preserved. Reinhard, along with other scientists, had hoped that Juanita's body had frozen immediately at the time of death and had stayed frozen. That would have preserved the nucleus of her cells, where her DNA is stored. DNA, a long molecule shaped like a twisted ladder, functions somewhat like the instruction manual for the body. It determines what each cell will become and do. It sends the messages that cause some cells to become brain cells, and others to become muscle cells. Your DNA determines if you will have blue or brown eyes; if you will have straight or curly hair; if you are likely to be tall or short. Your DNA comes from a combination of your mother's and father's DNA. Each of your parents inherited their DNA from their parents. That's why people who are related often look alike; their DNA is similar. By comparing the DNA of different people, scientists can tell how closely related they are.

When Reinhard first realized Juanita was frozen, he was thrilled because he thought her organs would have been preserved, as well as her cells and DNA. If that were true, scientists would be able to study Juanita's DNA to learn who her contemporary relatives are, where she came from, and possibly where the people in the Andes came from.

It appears this is not going to happen.

"We're hampered," Dr. McCarthy says, "by the fact that though on the surface she appears to be intact, a good bit of her tissues are really dissolved. It's going to be difficult, if not impossible, to isolate any DNA."

McCarthy and other researchers continue their efforts. And while they do, they learn more about Juanita.

And they ask more questions.

How She Died

How did Juanita die?

"Look at the skull," Dr. Fishman said, using his laser pointer to throw a red dot onto a movie screen that showed an X-ray image of Juanita's head. "We want to see how she died and what the circumstances around her death were."

We were in Washington, D.C., at the offices of *National Geographic* magazine for a press conference about the discoveries on Mount Ampato. After returning from his adventure on Ampato, Reinhard had called *National Geographic* for help in mounting a second expedition. He received an immediate yes. Within a month, he and Zarate, along with a team of

Geographic explorers and camera crew were back up on Ampato. At 19,200 feet, the team found the bodies of two more sacrificed children, a boy and a girl. Within the girl's tomb in the frozen earth, the team uncovered a wealth of Inca artifacts, including pottery, drinking vessels, spoons, textiles, and a small pair of sandals made of plant fibers and alpaca straps. The girl, who was perhaps eight when she was sacrificed, had probably taken the sandals with her as she was brought up the mountain.

Now, six months later, many of the people involved in the two Ampato expeditions were gathered to discuss their findings and theories. As Dr. Fishman spoke, Juanita sat propped up in a glass case within an even larger glass case in another room. A refrigeration unit filled the space between the two glass cases with moist, cold air, keeping her body from further decay. Computer-based controls constantly monitored the temperature and humidity of the unit. An alarm would sound if the temperature rose above 25° Fahrenheit.

Dr. Fishman had examined Juanita using CAT scans, a form of X ray, to look within Juanita's body without having to surgically cut her open. The CAT scans took X-ray photos in single slices—691 of them—which were then transformed by a computer into three-dimensional pictures.

"What we can do with a mummy," Fishman explained, "is cut through the mummy without having to do an autopsy."

Dr. Fishman pointed his red laser dot at a faint line near the right eye socket of Juanita's skull. "We can see a skull fracture," he pointed out.

New pictures appeared on the screen. The skull turned and we were now able to look within and see her brain.

"Here we can see the brain pushed over," he said. "And this was the cause of death. Intercranial bleeding."

She had been struck on the head, probably with a club, Dr. Fishman explained. As her skull fractured, she experienced bleeding and swelling that pushed her brain over and killed her.

The next day, newspapers printed the story that Juanita had been killed by a club. Yet, as other researchers continued their work, some questions began to rise.

Dr. McCarthy, the pathologist, expressed some doubt. Was she killed by a blow to the head?

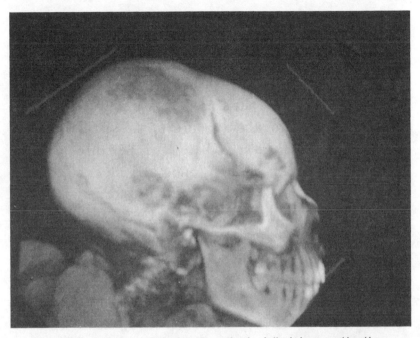

▶ *A CAT scan of the frozen girl's head reveals a crack in her skull, which was caused by a blow to the head. Was she struck before or after her sacrifice? Was it by a person or a falling rock? These questions have yet to be answered.* COPYRIGHT DAVID GETZ

"Well, it's hard to say," Dr. McCarthy explained. While we know her fracture was severe enough to kill someone, and that her brain was pushed over to one side, McCarthy was not sure if we had discovered the cause of death, or something that happened to her body after it died and was frozen for five hundred years.

"The lungs and all the organs seemed to be pushed over to one side," McCarthy explained. "I don't know what that means."

John Verano also has his doubts. "When I heard that, it didn't make any sense," Verano says. "The reason being that in these sacrifices, the sacrifice was supposed to be perfect." The Incas believed the gods required a perfect child. Writers just after the conquest describe how the Incas searched for physically perfect children for their sacrifices. Why would they bring such a child up the mountain and then damage her appearance?

Inca textiles were as significant to them as flags or religious articles are to us. If the Inca valued their textiles, why would they strike somebody on the head and risk having her bleed on these textiles? Though a head wound doesn't always bleed, and no blood was found on Juanita's clothing, Verano thinks striking a victim would have been inconsistent with the ways of the Incas, who most often buried their sacrifices alive.

Verano also wonders about Juanita's grip on her aksu. As a physical anthropologist, he knows that muscles constrict after death. The body naturally tenses. The appearance of a hand clenching something might just happen by chance. Still, it seems odd that

she would wind up looking as if she were clutching her clothing. It doesn't seem consistent with being struck on the head.

Bill Conklin also wonders.

"Her whole body looks as if she were cold," Conklin says. "Her arms are up close to her body. She has that huddled look a person gets if they're sitting there and it's very cold. And she very much has that feeling."

Could Juanita have frozen to death? Could her grip on her aksu be her last effort to keep herself warm?

It is a question that may never be answered. And it leads to many more. If we cannot know how she was killed, can we know why?

A World of Sacrifice

There has never been a place where we found so many sacrifices together," says Dr. Jane Pratt, an expert on the customs and religions of mountain people. Pratt says that we can assume something big and important must have been occurring.

But what could have been happening?

Daily life for common people of the Andes was filled with offerings. When farming, peasants poured chicha onto the ground as a gift to Pachamama, the earth goddess. At dangerous or important places on roads or mountain passes, travelers would find a pile of stones called an apachita. The traveler, asking the mountain god for protection, would add a stone to the pile or leave something small, such as a piece of torn clothing, some coca leaves, straw, an eyelash. This ritual is still common today in the Andes, and Reinhard always observes it when climbing.

The gods spoke through nature. If the gods were angry with people, they might cause a landslide, drought, or volcanic eruption. If the gods were pleased, they could send the rain, make the herds flourish, or display veins of gold and silver in the mountains. Since every aspect of their lives was controlled by the will of their gods, the Andean people were constantly trying to keep the gods happy. It was essential to always show appreciation and respect.

Perhaps the Incas believed the mountain gods were unhappy. Was a nearby volcano erupting? Even if the volcano was not spewing forth lava, its ash would pollute the water that ran down into the local villages. Was there a drought? Were there ground tremors hinting at a coming earthquake? In any of these situations, the Inca might offer Juanita and her companions to calm the mountain, to show it respect. Another possibility Pratt offers is that the Incas may have taken something of great value, such as gold or timber from the mountains. Juanita and the two other children might then be given as a gift in return.

What is the evidence?

▶ *The frozen girl, or Juanita, as seen through a glass case.* COPYRIGHT DAVID GETZ

Ampato was not snow-covered at the time of the sacrifices. While a modern climber is capable of ascending a snow-covered peak, great numbers of people carrying tons of supplies would not have been able to climb the mountain when it was covered by snow and ice. Snow-covered, frozen ground would have made it nearly impossible to dig the tombs of the other two children. Ice acts as a cement, turning soil and gravel into a mixture that is as hard to penetrate as a city sidewalk. The ground must not have been frozen when the children were first buried. The snow and freezing must have come later, after the bodies were entombed.

Why would Ampato not be snow-covered? Perhaps there was a drought. Or perhaps a volcano was erupting, littering the mountain with ash that melted the snow. Either a drought or a volcanic eruption would disrupt the water supply of the people in the valley. Their herds and their crops depended on the water coming down from Ampato. They would perceive either event as an angry message from the spirit of Ampato.

How could they erase that anger? How could they show their respect to Ampato? What gift could they offer the mountain so that it would once again send down its cool, clean water? How could they save their village?

Reinhard elaborates. The event would have involved more than just the presenting of a "gift" to the mountain. There would have been prayers to the sun god, the earth goddess, the other mountain gods. "But you don't climb to the top of a particular sacred mountain that's controlling livestock and crops to do something for the sun," Reinhard adds. "You can do that from down below. There was a reason to be on *that* mountain."

A Great Honor

Her people were suffering. Something terrible was happening. The mountain god was angry. Why? What could be done? The chroniclers tell us that priests might have cut open a llama and removed its insides to look for clues. They might have watched a fire of coca leaves, studied the behavior of animals, analyzed the movements of a spider in a jar.

At some point, they came to a conclusion: sacrifices needed to be made to the mountain. They would consult the ruling Inca.

A search began for a perfect child.

To be picked would be a privilege. "She certainly would have been willing," Dr. Pratt explains. "She was a gift from the whole people. And her sacrifice was meant to ensure the future of her people. To be specially chosen to be offered to a god was the highest honor the Inca could bestow."

"Did she fully understand that she was going to die? Did she believe she was going to have a wonderful afterlife?" Dr. Morris wonders. "I don't know. She certainly would have been aware that she was being very well treated, that she was important."

She was probably brought to Cuzco, where the priests began preparing her. She might have been asked to fast. Her textiles would be selected. At some point, she was returned to Ampato.

Her trip probably began with a parade of priests. Helpers led llamas carrying pottery, food, and items to be sacrificed. Villagers probably followed behind, singing and dancing until they reached the base camp at 16,300 feet. This camp consisted of a number of round and rectangular structures. There was a corral for the llamas.

The next day, the marchers climbed to 19,200 feet. If Juanita was fasting, she was most certainly becoming weak or faint. She was probably carried up the mountain. She wore moccasins that were delicate, light leather. "I cannot imagine them being used," Bill Con-

klin says. "She could not have climbed the mountain in her moccasins. They were like bedroom slippers."

The following morning, the priests prayed and offered the mountain food and drink. They continued up the mountain until they reached the lower, grass-carpeted plateau, which had already been prepared for them.

The next morning, she was probably given her last meal. "Inside her stomach we found various vegetable materials," Dr. McCarthy explains. Since food cannot stay in the stomach for more than six hours, this indicates that Juanita did not live many hours after this meal. She may have been given some chicha to drink. She must have been weak from fasting, from the high altitude. The alcohol would make her thoughts hazy.

After more prayers and ceremonies, the priests climbed to Ampato's summit.

At some point, someone took her long, dark, braided hair and tied it with a string to the back of her belt.

We do not know what happened next.

"Our role now," Dr. Pratt says, "is to protect and honor this child and what she represents. She is a gift from the mountain to us."

What can she teach us about the Incas, about the Andean people before the conquest? What benefits can she bring the people of today's Peru?

She has taught us to look at a mountain as a living being.

How will we benefit from this gift?

Bibliography

Begley, Sharon, and Shreiberg, David. "Children of the Ice."
  Newsweek 136, no. 19 (Nov. 6, 1996): 72.

Bernard, Carmen. *The Incas: People of the Sun.* New York: Harry
  N. Abrams, Inc., 1994.

Cameron, Ian. *Kingdom of the Sun God.* New York: Facts on File,
  1990.

Cobo, Father Bernabe. *Inca Religion and Customs.* Austin:
  University of Texas Press, 1990.

Cockburn, Aiden, and Eve Cockburn. *Mummies, Disease and
  Ancient Cultures.* Cambridge: Cambridge University Press,
  1992.

De La Vega, Garcilaso. *Royal Commentaries of the Incas.* Austin:
  University of Texas Press, 1966.

Hemming, John. *The Conquest of the Incas.* San Diego: Harcourt
  Brace and Company, 1970.

Mason, J. Alden. *The Ancient Civilizations of Peru.* London:
  Penguin Books, 1991.

Miller, Rebecca Stone. *To Weave for the Sun: Ancient Andean
  Textiles.* New York: Thames and Hudson, Ltd., 1992.

Minta, Steven. *Aguire.* New York: Henry Holt and Company,
  Inc., 1993.

Mosley, Michael. *The Incas and Their Ancestors: The Archaeology of
  Peru.* London: Thames and Hudson, Ltd., 1992.

Poma, Huaman. *Letter to a King.* Translated by Christopher
  Dilke. Written between 1567 and 1615.

Reinhard, Johan. "Peru's Ice Maidens." *National Geographic* 189, no. 6 (1996): 62–81.

———. "Sacred Peaks of the Andes." *National Geographic* 181, no. 3 (1992): 84–111.

Renfrew, Colin. *Archaeology.* New York: Thames and Hudson, Ltd., 1991.

Schuster, Angela. "Andean Ice Woman." *Archaeology* 49 (1996): 28.

Wilford, John Noble. "Mummy Tells Story of Sacrifice, Scientists Say." *New York Times,* 22 May 1996, sec. A, p. 13.

Index

(Page numbers in *italics* refer to illustrations.)